THE INSECURITIES OF MEN

Volume 3

Minister Isaac Wilson Jr.

Table of Contents

Introduction...4

Generational Curses...5

Evil Spirits and Good Spirits in the Spiritual Realms................8

Control Conscious...14

    Control...15

    Power..17

    Money...20

    Sex...25

Driven By Fear...29

    Fear of Failure...30

    Fear of the Unknown...30

    Fear of Rejection..31

    Lack of Confidence...32

    Negative Influence..33

    Comeback is Worse...34

    Decisions..35

    Deliver Us from Evil...37

Identity Crisis..46

    Mental Health..51

    Recognizing Your Insecurities.....................................54

Introduction

Firstly, I give all honor and praise to my Lord and Savior Jesus Christ. For without Him, I am nothing. The Lord our God reigns in heaven and on earth. He is our creator, and manufacturer of all creative beings.

Who better to know about the merchandise than the manufacturer? Who knows us better than the Lord Himself? If we desire change, we must first look to our Lord and Savior regardless of race, age, or sex.

Knowing who we are is a part of our changing. It is safe to say that we are always evolving or experiencing life situations that may not allow us to be the same spiritually, mentally, or sometimes physically.

We need to be secure with who we are. If we are not secure in who we are then we might not be able to handle situations and people in a mature or Godly way.

I am specifically dealing with men and their various insecurities in this edition. But we all know that certain matters could apply to women as well. Therefore, we are going to discuss the insecurities that most men have from a biblical perspective.

Generational Curses

A curse is a call for evil to come upon a person or a thing. To have a generational curse is to have that curse generate and develop in the origin of the family. In other words, that evil/curse is then passed down and through the family from generation to generation. Generational curse is unresolved sin in the family that must be broken by asking for God's forgiveness, and repentance of sin for that family. Otherwise, God's judgement will come upon you to address the sin in the family against him. (Numbers 14:18-23) Sin keeps us separated from God and causes us to make decisions, and lifestyle choices that can affect us and our family down the line. (Exodus 34:5-10) God created us as Tri-part beings meaning we have a spirit, soul, and body. (1Thessalonians 5: 23) Our flesh or body is constantly at war with our spirit to fulfill those urges, desires, and thoughts from our minds. (Galatians 6:8,5:17/Romans 8:5)There are certain behaviors, characteristics, and attitudes that we act out, due to those demonic forces assigned to us and our family by Satan. We must be reminded that these evil influences constantly try to attack and destroy us. The devil has a spiritual army, many of us are unaware about, and confused concerning various attacks against us. (Ephesians 6:10-18)

If you do not realize, we exist and live in a natural world; but we are truly spiritual beings having a natural experience. There is good and there is evil happening all around us. Have you ever asked yourself why does he or she, or even why do I act this way? Or why do I even do the things that I do?

It is quite simple. There are certain behaviors, characteristics, and even certain spiritual behaviors, certain spirits, or lifestyles that has been passed down from our forefathers. These familiar spirits oftentimes creep into the family through our grandparents or parents unknowingly and then are passed down to the next generation. For example, a prostitute can recognize another prostitute within a room full of other women; because of the spiritual identification within and upon them will connect the two. Rebellion against God is witchcraft. The devil uses manipulation and control to have us rebelling against the Lord through varies ways and people, which is witchcraft (Leviticus19:31 Isaiah19:3)

But knowing our family history gives us a better understanding of who we are and where we are going, or some sense of an identity. Not knowing who you are can also allow you to become insecure. Without knowledge of self, you will have an identity crisis and a lack of purpose in your life. These individuals seek status, love and a sense of belonging. Being able to accept who created you to be as a person, regardless of what people say, or think about you; is the beginning of being secure in YOU first. Many people are living their lives looking for certain people's approval. BIG MISTAKE, because you're opening yourself up to be manipulated and controlled by people, who really don't have your best interest at heart. If you really want to know who you are, Seek the Lord, and study his word (Holy Bible) The Holy

Bible is one of the most controversial books for thousands of years , because it's one of the most powerful weapons that we have to fight with in this spiritual warfare ;we daily encounter in this dark world we live in.(Psalms1:1-6,2Timothy3:16,Hebrews 4:12-13) It's a bad situation to not even know or have established relationships with your biological Father, Mother ,Sister ,Brother ,etc. This experience isn't a normal way of having family relations and what this does is, causes us to develop insecurities, when first developing relationships with other people. They'll be having trust issues, rejection, and not feeling good enough. Many of us men haven't dealt with a lot of our emotional hurts, pains and disappointments growing up. So, we just have become numb to them, and have many meltdowns that keep us from moving forward to become secure, and stable men. The devil has robbed us of the peace, happiness, joy, etc. growing up, without us even realizing it. This is why some are still boys in grown men bodies. All this unresolved anger, and pain has brought us is destruction and frustration with ourselves. Continue reading and you will no longer have to worry who is to blame for various troubles in our lives. It's not all on you, but some of it is, because some don't like to listen and respect authority either. You have rules and regulations everywhere, so if you weren't taught this at home, when you were young, trouble awaits you. (proverbs22:6) It's never too late for a person to be trained, or mature, but the many pitfalls would've been avoided, if you were trained up according to the principles of God's word. Sometimes you can train your kids up in that way, and they still decide to go a different route. That would be on them, as long as you've done your part as the parent. God gives us all a free will; he doesn't force us to do anything we don't want to do.

Evil Spirits and Good Spirits in the Spiritual Realms

There is a certain behavior that is evil; but easy for some individuals to do with enjoyment. They can not help themselves; and they do not know why they can not stop. You have some that may know; but do not have the power to stop or say no. We will discuss this later. But we must start opening our eyes, and allow God to reveal the traps and pitfalls being setup for us to fail, quit, and or give up (Daniel 10:13, Revelation12:7, Jude1:9)

Knowing the history of the family helps you understand what you are up against. You may not have made certain decisions if you understood who your enemy really was. (1Peter 5:8/Romans 8)

There is an army of wicked forces we are fighting against that seek to destroy us. We need to understand that Satan and his army's total mission is to kill, steal, and destroy. Some may ask what does Satan's army want to destroy, kill, and steal? Satan wants to steal your hopes and your dreams. He wants to kill your desire to live and he does so by attacking your body with sickness and eventually death. Satan wants to destroy our mind and he wants to steal our joy and happiness. Most importantly Satan wants to destroy our relationship and fellowship with God. (John 10:10, Luke11:24)

Many times, people lower their standards when they do not understand their history and other people before us historically who have made bad decisions. And I understand that some of us may or may not be able to get that information of the bad decisions/behavior of our fore-parents lifestyles; but it is worth the time and effort to investigate and look into it. But if not, ask God to reveal the demonic force or evil spirit that is running rampantly in the family. Older people back in the day didn't like to share various secrets with some family members. they were afraid or embarrassed, so some took those things to their grave. Extra marital affairs, substance abuse, racism, incest, molestation, homosexuality, abuse, murder, violence, stealing etc.

The thing that people must understand is that as long as you keep sinful acts hidden or buried then that evil spirit has been given permission to work its evil within the family from generation to generation. Evil spirits must be exposed and confessed specifically unto God. In other words, the current generations that are living must bring the sins of the fore-parents before God and ask God for forgiveness with a repenting heart and must denounce and renounce the sins of their ancestors. Repentance meaning a desire to change from within. Repentance means making a commitment to change in your heart and mind in order to change your lifestyle around; to a life that pleases the Lord Jesus Christ. As I've said before 'The Lord will never force us to change, he gives us all a free will to decide our paths. (Matt.12;34–45)

Expose those demons that have set trends in our lives unknowingly based on our upbringing or development within the home. Mostly, everything we will learn about life, people, and ourselves, should have been learned at home. What we do with what we developed from our upbringing is a whole different story. There are 6 basic things that we should've been taught growing up;1. Developing a Relationship with the Lord 2. Know how to express and demonstrate love 3. Respect 4. Discipline 5. Responsibility 6. Knowledge of Self. These 6 basic things will help you be a well-grounded secure man. But a person can't teach you anything they haven't learned, studied or experienced themselves.

There are some parents who will use God's way and then there are some who use their way. Most of the time those parents raise their children the way they were raised. Because for some, this is all they know based on their experience from their parents.

I say parent or parents because all households are not two parent households. There are some adults until this day, who are resentful towards one of their parents for how they were treated by them. But we have to understand because the parent/parents may have been unloved by their parents they can only do what they know, unless they are willing to give their burdens to Jesus, and allow the Lord to teach them (Ephesians 6:1-4).

During our upbringing is where values and morals should be developed. But this is where insecurities set in due to lack of confidence or fear of failure as a parent due to lack of knowledge; not visibly having a male influence in the home can have a great impact on the way the home is ran. God intended for the man to be the leader of the household.

And not necessarily singling any race out; but by me being a black man I realize that there is a significant amount of single parent homes without a male leader or role model today. Moreover, these same children that grow up in single parent homes without positive male figures are not interacting with positive men on a regular basis. Being up under women all the time isn't good for young boys, because they will start to develop female tendencies and start handling things like there Mom, Grandma, or woman would handle things. Some men don't know how to conduct themselves like real men; because they probably never had good examples from any men growing up. So some men grow up insecure of not knowing how to be a good father to their children. The feeling of being inadequate in certain areas of life may grab us all sometime. But there is freedom in being honest to yourself first. People will respect you more when you honestly, just say 'I Don't Know". Our egos as men will sometimes keep us in chains and make you old before your time. We all need somebodies help in our journey in life. This mentality of I don't need anybody's help is a trick of the enemy. Some of us are so lost and can't find our way back, because of your wrong perspective of life. The Lord has placed so many gifted people in this world to bless others. Some men are so competitive, we won't hear someone out, that God has placed in your path, to take you to a higher level in life. When you're secure in who you are, and honest with yourself, it won't bother you to ask a successful dude; 'How did you Accomplish That'? can you show me ,or teach me how to do the same thing? (Proverbs 27:17)

Many times, the men are absent fathers because they do not want to man up and take care of their responsibility as men. On the other hand, some of these same men choose not to be in the child's life because the relationship with the child's mother did not work out. Sometimes the fathers reject the child or put other things and people before their child. No wonder there are problems with raising our children today.

Let me say that it is possible for a single parent to take on the responsibility and role of both parents. But it takes a strong individual to do so. Yet, God intended for man and woman to raise a family as husband and wife.

But we do not live in a perfect world. Thanks be to God that he can make a crooked situation straight, if we let him know we are unprepared for certain things. We must seek God's wisdom; and knowledge so we do not have to be insecure men.

If we look within ourselves sometimes, we think that some situations are just too out of our control to be fixed. But if you trust in God and lean not to your own understanding, and acknowledge God in all of your ways then God will direct your path. On the other hand when your trust in God is not strong enough then you have to watchout because this is when the insecurities can creep into your mind, spirit, and into your life. (Isaiah 42:16-17/Proverbs 2:9-16)

Oftentimes those men who are raised by single parent women exhibit irresponsible behavior because they are used to their mother doing everything for them. Or some households may have mom and dad in the same home; but the dad exhibits lazy behavior. Some children that observe this lazy behavior from their fathers may think that this behavior is normal, and they use it as a blueprint of what a father 's role should be and do in the home. When this lazy behavior is exhibited by the father in the home, it allows and leads to the wife becoming the leader in the home.

Those who allow the woman to run the household are then henpeck; and the sons will seek a bossy woman of that stature. Only a bossy woman does not mind taking on both roles. However, on the other hand, some children do better with one parent in the home. It is a motivation for some people to beat the odds.

But we must train up a child in the way God intends for us to. Teach our children to choose the right group of people to associate with. Peer pressure exists with adults as well as children. You should not have to work so hard to feel special—because you are supposed to get that love and support from in the home and your family.

Some men work so hard to impress someone or a group of people to feel apart of something. Growing up feeling rejected in your home makes you feel tremendously insecure around your peers. I know some of us are raised to think and believe that if you express yourself and get emotional then you are weak.

But what you do not realize is bottled-up emotions gives Satan and his demons right to come in and torment and control your mind with wicked thoughts. Rejection is one of the things that may cause you to shed a tear. That is how deep it can be; but it cleanses you because you are dealing with the pain head on. Trust God for healing and restoration in your life to continue. Anything you hold that is evil within you gives the devil the right to come in to get what he wants and then uses it to his advantage. But you have to release any unforgiveness or evil thoughts that you may have by repenting to God and relenting the sinful behavior. (2 Corinthians 3:10).

Control Conscious

These traits are what most insecure men have and are very difficult to deal with, And At times very unreasonable, verbally and physically abusive. Extremely sensitive and have various complexes about themselves they're uncomfortable expressing to others. Some people are aware of their issues, but don't care and others aren't. They expect other people around them to put up with their attitude and behavior, because they believe they're not that bad. Or some believe there fine, and don't need healing and deliverance. The purpose of this chapter is to make you aware of the power of self-control. This is were being filled with the Holy Spirit is necessary to empower us to live a victorious life. Many of us don't believe we need salvation, until we reach a crossroad in our life. (1corinthians2:5) We can only be secure within ourselves, when we learn to trust and be secure in God. (Proverbs3:5) Complex means a related group of repressed or partly repressed emotionally significant ideas, which cause psychic conflict leading to abnormal mental states or behavior. In other words, many of us have held onto many things for a long time; of things we haven't accepted about ourselves. Or certain events or things that has happened to us, that we might not had control of concerning past events in our life. Many of us have mental states; that we need God's healing and deliverance from, to restore us to fulfill our purpose in life. (Romans 12:2) Control conscious makes us aware when were out of line, out of order, out of control. To the point where your beyond over the top. When your attitude about yourself and other people is unregulated and insensitive; your behavior will negatively affect those people around you. Some of us don't do a self-analysis regularly concerning our mental state to be aware of the changes in our attitudes more consistently. The battle always starts in our minds first (our thoughts, emotions, perception). we have to be conscious of what we're watching and listening to; so we can guard ourselves from demonic influences to attack us.

Control

Control is the power to give orders or to retain something—self-restraint.

Some men don't realize that using control to stroke their ego doesn't give them any power. When we understand whose really in control. And when we know how to walk in the power of God the way he truly wants us to; Then we can be victorious and can overcome all of the insecurities that the devil has tried to put upon us.

We must understand that there is a difference between the power of God and the power of the world. We must understand that the power of the world makes us believe that we are doing everything with our own ability and with our own intellect. But with the power of God, we must rely on having faith in God.

The power of the world is ruled by Satan; but it is not controlled by him. Understand that God has allowed the devil to rule over this world's system for only a short time; but God controls the whole world. (Luke 4:1-13)

We are under the control and influence of the devil when we start believing that we do not need the Lord. When we think that we do not need the Lord then God shows us just how much we need Him. The clout, the status, the king; all titles that men chase because we want acceptance, popularity, and most importantly for some "I am somebody" is what power signifies to some. with all the power that Jesus had to help him get off the cross, when he was being crucified is amazing to me. But what that's called is meekness. Meekness means power under control, because he knew God the Father's purpose and desire was to deliver us from eternal Hell by sacrificing his life for us. (John3:16) Jesus could've flexed his muscles to prove to people the power he had, but God's plan had to be fulfilled. He was born to Die. And because he was resurrected from the dead, so shall we also who have accepted him as their personal savior. (John11:17-27)

Some men have been verbally abused all their lives and told they would never be anything good to the point where they start believing those things. They do all manner of things to prove to themselves and others they were wrong. But a lot of them do not understand that during those processes of thought, they are being influenced and controlled like a puppet by the devil. This is how violence in our world starts, by trying to get revenge and even with people, amongst other things. Our desires can consume us if they don't line up with the will of God. Oftentimes God allows things to happen in our life, which is God's permissive will, but not necessarily God's perfect will for our life. (Hebrews 10:23-32) (Job1:1-12)

There are three things that often causes men to lose control of themselves: It's power, money, and sex. In fact, some of them do not know what a real man is or supposed to be. They do not know what a real man is supposed to be because they have never seen the attributes of a Godly man exhibited in their home or life. everyone may define success differently.

Power

Power– 1. The ability or capacity to do something or act in a particular way. 2. The capacity or ability to direct or influence the behavior of others or the course of events. There's a price you must pay for power, and that's called accountability, and some suffering. The reason why some of our young people can't get it together is because some of the older generations have used their influence and guidance upon the younger people to make wrong decisions in their lives. Some of our young people hold our older, experienced people in high regard because they're searching for answers, to be lead in the right direction. It's not God's way to mislead someone, just to meet your agenda or plans; because you know these individuals hold you to the highest esteem to do right by them. (Luke12:42– 49) For some men certain levels of power gives them a feeling of satisfaction within themselves. Some just want the position of Power; not concerned about anything else, if the focus and attention are directed towards them. Certain status makes them feel like they've achieved greatly or are so special to people. If you don't know or already feel this way prior to being in that position, will step on people to get there and stay there. You can't allow certain levels of power, or influence in life go to our heads. This is where the devil will come and influence us with jealousy, and murder. These two evil forces work together. Devil doesn't care if he uses a family member or a friend in your quest for power; to take someone out. (Genesis 4:1-14) In your evil quest for power; you begin to mistreat people, take advantage, or look down on people. They become arrogant, rude, and disrespectful towards people. They easily forget the struggles they've experienced before their current high position. But when the Lord brings you to a certain place of power or higher position in life; it's for you to glorify him and not yourself. (romans12:3-8) When God promotes you to a certain place in life, you don't have to worry or stress about anyone taking that from you. He blessed you with That.

So, We take on jobs as supervisors, policeman, congressman, pastors, CEO, President of different organizations to flex our muscles. Sometimes these individuals that seek these positions sometimes abuse their authority. These individuals do not realize that God is their boss above all, and they will have to answer to Him. Some of them are using their authority for all the wrong reasons. Romans 9:17/Colossians 3:22-25

What I am saying is that we should walk in the power and the authority that God has called us to, but due to the lack of knowledge of taking our rightful place in the home, marriage, and life itself we're confused. Seek God's wisdom first, and he'll lift you up beyond what you can ask or think. (Ephesians 3:20) We develop these insecurities and because of those unresolved insecurities in men they oftentimes abandon their responsibilities, shutdown and quit. Sometimes abandoning the homes where their children reside.

Not having an example or role model teaching us how to lead, is hard for some men to take their place. Because of our insecurities as fathers, sons, husbands, and brothers the women are left struggling for stability in their households. Jesus said if you want to be great learn how to be a servant. The way how you obtain power, influence, attention, and popularity. Get back in your role as a father to your children; co-parenting investing your time and energy in your family, is more than anything money can buy. Use your God given gifts to serve the people in your community and around you. The devil has convinced some men to believe, I will get respect, influence, by showing other guys how tough, and hardcore I am. Or how much money I'm making, how many women have, and the expensive cars I drive. Material things don't bring happiness or inner peace all the time. Some of us suffering a lonely, unhappy miserable life, because we don't know the Lord, your creator and manufacturer (mark 10:42-45)

Money

1Timothy 6:10

The Bible states that the love of money is the root of all evil. So money itself isn't evil, but many of our evil intentions to obtain money is the problem for many people. The things that money influences and makes people do are amazing. Money allows you to obtain all the material things of this world; but how were able to obtain those things is what concerns God. we must always remind ourselves of the fact that money is merely a piece of paper, but with that being said ;How is it that people are willing to sell their souls to the devil for a piece of paper ? The devil already knows those people who value that piece of paper more than themselves. And Satan plots to rob you of your self-worth, and identity. From here your focus will be on you seeking approval from other people, your value and worth. There is a price you must pay to be rich the thing with riches, some praise and worship their riches and not the Lord. The bible says 'you can't serve two masters. God gives you a choice if you want to worship him or mammon (Matthew6:24) You can have quantity, but no quality of life. Some men are rich, but very unhappy because there is no relationship with God. There will always be an emptiness inside of you that money can't accommodate. Material things cannot keep you happy, but for a short time. then you see something else that is newer and much better than you purchased. You'll never really be content or satisfied without a connection with God. When it comes to money, many people don't know how to separate their needs from their desires. Many people are in debt and can't get ahead; because they want things, they don't necessarily need. Wrong intentions, and motives are another way we get ourselves in trouble financially. Your attitude and way of thinking will make you or break you. For example, are you wanting something because some of you were able to buy it? Do you want to buy something, to make people think you have money? We have to think about these things, when we feel so compelled to spend money on something we really can't afford. We have to honestly analyze our intentions, and thoughts before spending unnecessarily. If we want God's blessings we have to deal with certain areas in our heart and mind, so we can be completely delivered to avoid putting ourselves in debt and depression. (Psalms1:1-6) It's ok to have nice things, but we can't allow nice things to have us out of control; in debt and lacking. Some of us emotionally spend money to make us feel better about ourselves. Then when you don't have anything left, you will start making risky decisions to survive. Another thing we must know is what's a priority and what's not. Pay attention to what you're spending your money towards. From here you must plan and make some decisions, what you want to do to improve your money issues. Develop a plan to save, or cutback on various unnecessary expenses. Prepare yourself to be able to gain more money through various classes, certifications; that can build a portfolio of various skills you can offer a company: or self-employment. Time is money, the same people who waste money, also waste a lot of time making excuses about something they could've been accomplished. Many men have gotten tricked to believe fast money is good money. Lots of risks comes with fast money; but the devil tries to trick us to believe we can pull it off. Forgetting about those jealous people around that you, must contend with. Also, the betrayal around; of some people you'll face will keep you from getting far with that fast money. We all know what fast money I'm referring to that has landed millions of men behind bars or murdered out in these streets for decades. Satan has convinced so many men that a life of crime is the only way you can provide for yourself and family. He doesn't want you to know that God has put gifts and talents in you to fulfill your purpose in this life. You don't have to be out here lost and unhappy doing what you're doing ,to so called survive out here, working dead end jobs. God has better for you, he'll reveal it once you reconnect yourself to him. (Proverbs 18:16) The devil has tricked you to do his dirty work, where you've ignored the gifts and treasures that God has installed in you. But Satan blinds our eyes to keep us chained to him; so, we can't be free or give God the glory for how great he created you to be a blessing in other people's lives. Even when you were in your mother's womb, God had a purpose and great plan for your life. (Jeremiah1:5/Psalms 139:13) Some men steal money, sell drugs, pimp women; and manipulate people to gain money, but that's why you 're always looking over your shoulder. This was not God's purpose for men to be successful. People with this criminal mindset don't understand a man who's going to work, trying to make an honest living. They think a working man is a weak sellout or an Uncle Tom. These insecurities come in when we feel like this is all I know how to do, to support my family. This is called growth change, because from here, we will be prepared be able to trust God at his word to supply all your needs and desires. (Phillipians4:19/Psalms 37:4)

Any successful and prosperous or wealthy person understands that changes must occur in order to elevate to a higher level. Some men must change their level of thinking in order to receive all that God has for them. it is only so much you could handle if you are at a certain level. Some men want more money but cannot handle the responsibility of what more money brings (Psalms 37:4). The real reason why some people really will never reach that level of prosperity and wealth is because their motive is not right.

This is when and where that change can take place. When we are honest with God and let God know the desires of our heart and be sincere with God then and only then can God take us to the next level spiritually, emotionally, and financially. What some men do not realize is that God is not going to bless you just to benefit you God knows if you had a million dollars who you would give to or who you would be a blessing to because Gid truly know your heart. A lot of us want to show off getting a lot of attention and start forgetting about God (John3:16).

A lot of people who are rich have this problem-- they feel like they can buy their way to heaven they don't need a blessing from God, or they start taking credit and pets themselves on the back for what they have obtained. Some put their trust in their riches and material things but the wealthy and prosperous put the trust in God but if it had not been for God himself and the relationship, they have with him they would not have what they have what many of us as men do not understand is that God is no respecter of person.

Your time will come too for a wealthy and prosperous life if you can continue to seek the Lord. You do not have to get jealous because you do not make more money than someone else or that your significant other makes more money than you, Put the insecurities to rest men. We need to stand in our position as men. Real men do not try to compete with women.

There are many men that have money; but are very lonely because they do not have genuine friends. They say when you have money you have a lot of friends. Some people realize that everyone is your friend when they can get something out of you. When God bless you, He will let you know who is really on your side and He will let you know who to trust. When you begin to realize that when God bless you with something you do not have to worry about someone stealing or losing what God has blessed you with.

Many men seek to have more money for security within themselves. Oftentimes when you have a lot of money the world thinks highly of you. However, when you become a seeker of money this leads to insecurities. If you are not careful chasing after money can make you cocky, arrogant, and prideful. Please do not get caught up with associating yourselves or having so called friends who are insecure. Some people who are insecure can be very negative thinkers and quitters. It is best to associate yourself with the Most High and trust in God first before you put your trust in money.

They will never reach a level of prosperity until they change their way of thinking. They allow jealousy to come in because they believe that they can not achieve certain milestones in their life. God will not allow money to be your God while serving Him. Money does not solve all the problems in life. It is a resource that God provides for us for food, clothing. and shelter. As men we should direct our focus towards God. Everything else will fall in line and God will prosper you.

Sex

It is an appetite that can become an addiction—just like anything else. When we understand the intent of God's plan for sex, we will realize that we have misused sex and abused it (1 Corinthians 13:1-13; 1 Corinthians 6:12-18), it has come to a point where, some men aren't even considering marriage anymore. Some just want to just casually have sex without any strings attached. But sex has a deep spiritual connection beyond what we can imagine.do you realize that every woman you slept with you married them. Every life is birthed into this world through their mother's womb (Genesis 2:21-24/Mark 10:6-10) Sex is very powerful act to just casually perform with any and every one ,because spirits can transfer through sex and attach themselves to us. Therefore, for some men, it's a game, or it gives them a feeling of self-esteem to see just how much sex he can have with various women. It gives some men a sense of security, power to know they have slept with several women. Just think about how you are having sexual relations with so many women, may have altered your future. Now you have kids your responsible for unexpectedly now. Sex was initially created by God for married people to build the institution of family. Genesis 9:1-9There are so many children in foster care, or who are being raised by so many different other people than their biological parents. Kids didn't ask to be here, and the Lord still can still work those things out in favor of those kids. When we deviate from God's instruction's, sometime there are different consequences we must deal with for the rest of our lives. We live in sex crazed society; that's all you ever hear or see over social media, TV, Radio, etc. Our young generation of kids are so exposed to all these immoral, wicked, perverse things daily. It's amazing how times have changed and evolved over the decades. Young females are having babies at a very young age. Young men are becoming father's before they reach the age of adulthood. We must understand that everything God has created, the devil will try to pervert it. Perversion means 1. The alteration of something from its original course, meaning, or state to a distortion or corruption of what was first intended. 2. Sexual behavior or desires that is considered abnormal or unacceptable.

Sometimes our attractions are more than physical, they are more spiritual than most men realize. For example, a woman who has a lustful spirit as you, will be attracted to you. Here you are caught up into how good you look, an how well dressed you are. Those familiar spirits will have you feeling and thinking, you've known each other for years. With this—sometimes we think we have a secure friendship and or relationship; but for a woman to give her body to you through sex is very powerful. For women they must feel a connection with you more emotionally, spiritually before they decide to be with you on a intimate level, unless she's a prostitute. Men are wired a little differently, we are more visual, meaning any woman were attracted to; we can have sex with them without any consideration for a long-term commitment. When we do things contrary to what God says in his word; people are hurt, and damaged in many ways.

When we realize the many lives we've affected as a result of our sexual appetite, sometimes it is too late, but with some men it is about our egos. These things: power, money, and sex—mainly feed our egos.

Power and money can tear a relationship apart; high sex drive and greed can destroy any marriage if you allow it. Because some men have so many past sexual experiences that comes back to haunt us, if we haven't been delivered, cleansed from all those other women or men attached to you from the past. So, some of us have brought our sexual luggage's with us from the past into our new relationships and marriage. You trying to figure out what's their problem, but the whole time it's you, who needs the healing and deliverance. Many men have been affected by sexual greed and fetishes. Some men have been sexually abused, molested, raped, or been in a bad relationship that has affected their whole outlook on sex. Consequently, their whole sexual experiences afterwards have been awkward and abnormal to them.

Some men are insecure with their sexuality and are afraid to discuss or ignore it as a result of various experiences. Some men hide these things from their mates and do not reveal these things to people who can be affected by their behavior (Ephesians 10:17). This is why some men have sexual identity issues; Meaning one minute they want to deal with women, and other times they want to engage in sexual activities with men. Some men have experienced some traumatic experiences sexually in their lives that may have never really been addressed.

Call on God for your deliverance. You have been disguising things long enough. Some men will even try to sleep with several women to validate that they are heterosexual. But there is deliverance and healing that must take place with being taken advantage of as a man. Only God has the power to heal these things in our lives, nothing else can do it. Or there is a demonic spirit in your family, such as homosexuality that has gone from one generation to the next. Some of these men who experience these things don't talk much about them. Fear and shame is what the devil has used to keep them in chains all there lives. They will consume you and steal your sexual identity, if not confronted and dealt with. Healing and deliverance is a priority; sweeping these things under the rug will only make matters worse, internally for victims. This will hinder you from expressing and demonstrating love. Because it's a internal wall they have built up to prohibit people from getting too close to them. What's even hurtful for some victims, is the fact that it was a family member you loved and trusted; that took their innocence and manhood from them. When God forbids us to do something, it's for a reason or purpose we don't always understand. But the Fear of God is where we grow as a person. This is another reason why so many people are infected with STD's, because of our sex crazed lifestyles. Please read this chapter in the bible where certain sexual relations God forbids us from having (Leviticus 18/Galatians 5:13-26) for us to overcome these sexual strongholds, we need to ask for God's forgiveness and repent. Allow God to be Lord over your life and accept his son Jesus Christ as your personal savior. It's vital to ask God to fill you with the Holy Spirit, with the evidence of speaking in tongues. Also fasting and praying, against those urges and desires our bodies crave. Reading and meditating on God's word is necessary just like food is for our body. It's food for the mind, spirit, and body. (1john 1:9/mark9:17-29/Acts2:1-20/Matthew 4:4/Psalms 119:11/2 Corinthians6:6/John14:16-26. Find you a good church home, where the Word of God is preached, so you can grow and turn your life around. It's never to late to change your life around. Sometimes the sacrifices we make when we love someone and yourself are worth it. Our children need us Men, your wife or kid's mom needs you to give that child an opportunity we might not had from our fathers.

Driven By Fear

To be driven by something involves being controlled or motivated by something. This is where you can tell where and what people passions are (2 Timothy 1:7). But fear happens to be one of those things or influences that keep us bottled up with insecurities.

Fear is an emotional reaction that is unpleasant caused by nearness of danger or expectations of pain. The devil uses fear in so many ways to keep people enslaved physically, spiritually, and mentally. This subject is too vast to cover it all; but we will cover some aspects of it in this chapter. Fear keeps you stuck in the same position, so you cannot move forward.

The source of fear is not from God. You must understand that to know where the problem could be rooted. Many women do not realize that you can not be much of a support to your man unless you understand what his fears are. He may know what his fears are; but may not feel comfortable expressing them to you based on the attitude of the woman's attitude and spiritual growth. So those men fight with those insecurities all by themselves not understanding and being misunderstood by their significant others.

Fear does not come from God; it comes from Satan who will try to influence us to make bad decisions. Who will try to influence us to make bad decisions. We must deal with those thoughts, as soon as it comes into your mind. It is where our warfare starts; but if you do not know what God's word says then you are no match to fight the devil in the spirit realm (2 Corinthians 10:1-5); (Matthew 4:1-11). You must speak God's word out of your mouth in order to fight against the devil.

These are a few fears that we allow to control us as men:

1. Fear of failure
2. Fear of the unknown
3. Fear of rejection

Fear of Failure

Fear of returning to a previous position from your past. Some of us men have been told by people that we would never succeed. We would not accomplish our goals that we pursued for us. Your relationships would not last. Sometimes people tend to believe things that they hear repeatedly over a period of time.

Fear of the Unknown

Sometimes the current circumstances can get the best of some of us—not knowing what is at the end of the tunnel. Beating yourself up about past mistakes and decisions makes you feel like a failure or a loser. Change is a big part of that unknown. It is not always easy; but it is necessary sometimes. We will experience changes throughout our life. Learn to embrace it and trust in God for great results.

Fear of Rejection

Maybe you were rejected by someone you thought you were supposed to be together with or gotten married and it never happened. She did not want you anymore. For some—a father or mother disowning you as their child. Growing up you were treated as an outcast. People do not like your personality, or you are just different than some of your peers at school, work, church, or whatever.

Ask yourself what your fears are; and ask God for forgiveness, repentance; deliverance. Maybe you will be able to love yourself first. The fact is you must be able to love yourself before you can love anybody else. The devil is causing you to be unlovable to others and yourself. Now is the time for tables to turn for the better.

When you can love yourself, you will know how to love others. Perfect love cast out all fear (1 John 4:18). A woman can not love her man; and be afraid of him at the same time. Because he's insecure; he abuses her physically, verbally, and later after treating her this way he says he loves her. That kind of love does not grow—that is control and manipulation. Being insecure has a lot to do with being able to trust someone. Always thinking people are against them, so they feel like the only way to trust someone is by trying to control people through manipulation.

You can not have a mind of your own with an insecure man. He wants to keep you in a child-like state. Verbal abuse with the word love used so loosely to deceive them. Be able to recognize genuine love by spiritual character demonstrated. When you are at your weakest—you tend to let things get by you sometimes. Ordinarily you would have picked up on it—until things begin to get bitter. Or if you play around with this person, they will continually try you or kill you. Control and manipulation are a form of witchcraft.

Lack of Confidence

Confidence is a feeling of certainty, self-realization, and boldness. It is very important to have a good support group around you. It allows you to build upon your strengths and weaknesses. It gives you the confidence on how to view yourself and how to view others. Insecure men will not know how to view themselves nor will they know how to view others. When you can not trust yourself, you are not going to trust others. Some insecure men do not have a good support group. When I say support group, I am referring to family members, friends, co-workers, or parents.to encourage you toward your goals, dreams, and destiny (Psalm 131:1–23).

Confidence can develop with time. For some it is quicker to love confidence than gain it. Here is when your relationship with God should become necessary because God empowers us above our own abilities. Insecurities drop when God can get you to focus on his abilities rather than your own. It seems like the closer you get to the Lord, the more people will move away from you. The people begin to move away from you because they are not able to identify with the change taking place within you and with your new lifestyle. You will have to put your reputation on the altar to please God. No longer should you worry about what people think or feel about you. It is about how God feels and think about you. (Romans 12:2).

We spend precious time and money on education and qualifications to get us to that level where we will feel more confident in ourselves. Don't get me wrong—it is nothing wrong with educating yourself or gaining knowledge. Just remember that God does the qualifying and promoting you to the next level.

We can rest assured that when God has his hands on a situation or on an individual you can walk boldly with confidence, knowing that everything is going to work out for your good. The Lord wants all of us—not some of us. You will know when you have given the Lord all of you. You will trust Him even when you can not see your way during your trial and tribulations (1John 4:4).

People that are insecure will always try to make people think they have a lot of money or up there with the status quo. When you follow Christ—He will make people respect you because of the Godly character in your heart; especially when you realize God lives inside you.

Negative Influence

There is an old saying, "birds of a feather flock together". We need to be very careful about the company we keep. Sometimes you are judged by the company you keep. People who have the same thought capacity or familiarity of spirit will click and swear you are greatly connected.

When two individuals do not share the same interest there is confusion and chaos all due to insecurities about the disinterest. When you are confident in who you are and love yourself, then you are not easily influenced by negative influences. Anyone that pressures you to do something you do not feel like you should be doing or know that it's wrong, this is a negative influence.

Anytime you have to work that hard, where your soul is being drained to be a friend or just letting a person in your space; Beware because you have a demon of manipulation that is operating against you. They operate based upon how they can use or free load off someone. They see what you have to offer to benefit them. Therefore, the demon uses them to become a negative influence on you, if you are not careful. They can always sense when someone is desperate for a friend or are lonely. Moreover, people that are jealous hearted never have anything positive to say to encourage anyone.

Comeback is Worse

Demons will feel like you have something that belongs to them. Resist the devil and he will flee (2 Peter 17:22; Matthew 12:22-45). They will come back stronger to possess and influence you again. So please try to stay away from those types of people who mean you no good. When you are walking in fear or motivated by fear then negative influences can possibly affect you. Due to your insecurities—whatever influences you were under will make or determine what kind of behavior you demonstrate publicly. When the Lord delivers us, we must keep our deliverance. Do not think that it does not make you exempt from being attacked by these same demonic forces that had you in chains previously. Deliverance is a constant fight to keep from being in bondage.

Decisions

Decision is making a reasoned judgment abut something and the ability to form clear opinions and act on them. One of the ways to discover or know where some men's level of maturity is.

by their wrong decisions. There are maybe certain levels of making wrong choices. First, when you talk about choices—you are talking about having alternative routes. When you talk about making decisions you have narrowed your choices and are ready to set on that one decision. People are destroyed for a lack of knowledge.

There are some of us who are so insecure within ourselves that we do not know how to make decisions. We make wrong decisions because we do not know what God's will for our lives is. If you do not know what His will is' it is in the Holy Bible.

What He desires for us? Some may know His will; but choose to do what they want to do. When you do not have a plan or seek God's wisdom you will be lost, stuck, and afraid. Some of us men have wasted our youth away. When you get older you are not able to do a lot of things physically when you were younger; but God has the last word on everything (James 1:5). God gives us the victory when we consistently call on His name and when we consistently keep His commandments and do His will (Psalms 119:11).

When we realize how much our decisions can affect our family and people around us, we would think twice or ten times before we make the wrong decision. Men that are insecure tend to make emotional decisions, that maybe hard to keep them on the right track. We must realize that emotions can trick us to believe something that may or may not exist. Satan knows how to speak to our minds in the area of our emotions to persuade us and before we know it we are yoked into bondage. When we allow Satan to influence us then we have given him control over our minds.

I want people to realize that knowledge is power. Knowledge awakens our hearts and our minds to the plan that God has for us. If we truly want deliverance, we must repent and ask God for forgiveness and we have to turn away from the sin and turn away from the bad behavior. We must ask God to come into our hearts and fill us with His Holy Spirit (Mark 1:8).

The Holy Spirit will give you the power to keep your deliverance. He will give you the power to walk and talk right before the Lord. The Holy Spirit will give you the power to be all you can be in God's Army. You must take authority over the demon of fear, doubt, and control which can be the main evil forces you specify in your prayers to come against (Luke 1:35).

Know who your enemy is because Satan has an army as well (Ephesians 6:1-6). If you realize that sometimes Satan has put or sent those demons on assignment to you and your loved ones (Job 1:6-12). Look at your family history and the downfall of the men in your family and you will realize what has happened. Let us break the cycle and break the generational curses in Jesus' name. We must begin to call

all these plagues and curses out by name. Make these curses step down and resign and leave in Jesus' name and never return.

You must identify the area of struggle and you cannot indulge in the sin or entertain it because those demons that left may try to come back. If you sin by doing the same old things, then you are giving the enemy every right to come back. They will feel like you have something that belongs to them. Resist the devil and he will flee. (James4:7)

One of the biggest problems that we as men face and which may be another root cause for insecurities of men is what define us as a good man, a successful, prosperous man. We as men desire others to see us as such and even we ourselves desire to see ourselves as such. This is a question mark that we have in all of us; but here is what God says (Matthew 6:33; Psalm 1:10).

What is a real man? Based upon some of the answers is probably why some men are very insecure and unstable. A real man is one who loves God, serves God and others. God is the one who created you. He is our manufacturer (Genesis 1:27).

Deliver Us from Evil

I must say that black men may not be the only men who may have dealt with systemic racism, discrimination, or hardships coming up and through life. But I am speaking from my experience and knowledge coming up in an urban area in Washington, D.C.in the early 1980s and 90s. Some points that have been made could apply to anyone regardless of culture, race, or background. I would like to make that clear moving forward.

Everyone has a story; but as a black man there are some things that I have witnessed—globally of the injustices of some black people. Our history as black people in America should never be ignored or forgotten. Despite over four hundred years of slavery, oppression, suppression, and depression; it's amazing how some black men have had the resiliency and fortitude continuously to become successful. Despite it all many black people have made great contributions in building this great U.S.A. through the grace of the Lord. In the Lord 's prayer there is a part that says, "Deliver Us from Evil" (Luke 1:11; Romans 12:21).

We need to know that there is an ongoing battle of good and evil consistently taking place in the spiritual realm of this world that cannot physically be seen. You know that these evil spirits are around and exist in various forms like racism and violence. The evil works and acts of racism is a learned behavior. Right and wrong are taught to us and it is up to us, to consciously and morally make the right decisions. Often many of the decisions that people make are based upon their background and what was taught to them early in life.

This makes me raise a question: Are we as black people completely free? The way I see it, there is a system that is in place in our minds developed by our parents; and the world's system itself that has governed us and has caused major issues for us. God has left His Holy Bible for us as a manual on how to live on this earth. One of the many reasons people have considered God's word, "The Holy Bible", as the most controversial book throughout the centuries of times. On the other hand, many biblical prophesies have been fulfilled and are still being fulfilled today. It is important to study the word for yourself instead of going by what other people say (2 Peter 1:11–21; 2 Timothy 4).

The devil uses many ways to keep us blind from the truth and to keep us in bondage by him. The devil tries to keep your mind occupied by things that are not important. Back in the day. it was a thing that my peers and I would say, "If I make it to see 21 years old it would be a blessing". Back then Washington, D.C. was the murder capital of the world. At that time the statistical data was showing that D.C. was the murder capital of the world. Many news articles were proving that young black men were dying by the hand of gun violence daily. Statistics slated young black men at that time to be dead or in prison, before age 21. Ultimately, It is not how society views us; but it is rather how we view ourselves individually. if you view yourself or think of yourself negatively then how can you expect other people to view you any differently?

Once the enemy has you thinking bad and feeling bad about yourself—you are going to start acting out all that negativity. You have allowed the enemy to sink down into your mind and heart. You have allowed these negative words to influence you or possess you. If you believe everything negative that is said to you then, it can have a negative Impact on you (2 Corinthians 10:4-6). It is important to know what God says about you in His word. You must know that His word is a weapon to help you fight against the devil and his army (Hebrew 4:12-13). You must speak God's word daily over your life.

When you take possession of all that negativity—you become the owner or recipient of these curses spoken to you. You are not even aware that people have been planting evil seeds, against you and speaking curses on you. One of the main reasons you have accepted some of the negativity and verbally abusive words towards you because it came from someone you thought who truly loved you. This is why you were vulnerable enough to accept and believe the garbage, abuse, and curses that were spoken from them. It is said that "love will cause you to be blind" to certain things. Even sometimes through various trials and tribulations you have experienced.

This may have caused a deep wound that has hurt you to the point where you can not trust anyone. Especially if it came from a person who was supposed to be for you—like a parent, sibling, grandparent, or a long-time friend. Consequently. It causes you to withdraw and to be untrusting towards or in many relationships. You figure it is no one left to trust or embrace you—and not reject you. However, you can listen to what Jesus says about these so-called family members and friends.

Some men are at the last call for help and assistance to get back on their feet. We look to our government for help. They want you to be completely down and out before they try to give assistance. All this does is put your back against the wall and a hard place—to make tough and hard decisions in order to survive.

I have watched our government transport thousands of illegal migrants into the United States and provide housing, food, and monetary gains provided to them with taxpayer dollars. Meanwhile, there are thousands of American citizens that are still homeless with no health care and without food, housing.

Deliver us from evil Lord. The government already knows what people do—especially minorities and financially challenged do; when faced with severe hardship and struggles to make ends meet. They resort to a life of crime, drugs, and violence. If you already grew up in an unstable environment, it is easy to revert or conform to a lifestyle you had no choice to adopt for survival—after a period. Your perspective on life, other people, and yourself must change in order to make the right decisions in life. Otherwise, you will continue to make the same choices because your outlook and perspective remains the same (Romans 12:2).

You see, change must start in you—before thinking the other person must change. Oftentimes, the other person involved will think that your perspective is the only one that needs adjustment. Everyone needs to know that God is the creator and that He created everyone different. God created everyone with various cultures, backgrounds, and skin color.

No two people will have the same upbringing. In other words, you can have five children in the same household and if you interview them, they will have different perspectives and views on how they were raised. Know that everyone's upbringing will be different and know that everyone's values are not the same. And you must be mature enough to know this, understand this, and respect it.

I am very tired of hearing and seeing my black people killing and destroying one another. Black men are on the verge of extinction because of the use of drugs, crime, violence, and mass incarcerations, irresponsibility, and homosexuality. Lord deliver us from evil.

Some of this you can not blame all on the government system or racism. You are responsible for all your decisions as well. We must make better choices and take advantage of those opportunities given to you.

There are more drugs, guns, and violence in our communities. More jails are being built, and same sex relationships cannot reproduce children. These issues are leading to the extinction of the black population. Not to mention babies having babies.

All of these issues are plaguing the black community and what is even worse is the sad fact of black-on-black crime. It is a sad commentary that these same individuals do not think before making a bad decision like murder. They fail to realize that when you choose to murder someone—you take a life, and you will lose your life behind bars forever. It is sad to see so many lives ruined and gone away with great potential over the silliest and pettiest things. Jealous and hating on each other. But to look at the point of view from a spiritual side—all this violence and negativity plagues the black community because individuals are not aware that God is no respect of persons. Meaning just because you see someone doing well at the time, it could be their season that God decided to bless them. We all will have our harvest, that God has for us if we're patient enough to wait. Even more, some individuals are not aware that they are special in the eyes of God. Your season of greatness will come to you. You must be patient men (Deuteronomy 10:17; Romans 3). No one is more superior or better than the next person. Measure yourself to Christ and His righteousness.

You would be surprised of the amount of people who will do a lot of silly things—just for attention and recognition. Many times, when people act out—it is a sign that a person is lonely or searching for someone to show them some love, appreciation, and attention. We all have seasons in our lives; but it is important to know and understand what season we are in at that moment. The Lord promised to never leave us or forsake us. Being patient and leaning on God builds character in us (Hebrew 13:1-8; James 1:1-12).

Some of you may be going through a lot; and your circumstances may be dictating and controlling you to the point where you do not see a way out of your situation. You may be walking in the manner without form and direction from the Lord that can create a dangerous lifestyle for yourself. When you are going through trials and tribulations it sometimes draws people closer to God. But most times, we try to find various ways to cope with our pains and frustrations in life. Trying to evade these hurts and pains in your life is usually where many of our addictions originate from. Indulging in various vices—trying to avoid or medicate the stress, pains and hurts in your life. Guess who will step in and offer you all the wrong solutions? —the devil. He knows your poor choices can possibly steal, kill; and destroy your life. That is his job. He will use hurt people to wound and hurt someone else or even worse (Job 1:6-8; John 10:10; 1 Peter 5:8).

You do not hear about too many other ethnic groups killing one another in this country—like Black folks. If we ever decide to unite as a people, we would be a serious threat in this country. Many of us are intelligent, inventors, and great thinkers. Too bad many of us do not see ourselves that way. Many of us are in prison in our mind and do not even realize it. All of the Black-on-Black crime that the government refuses to do anything about it-- is a silent and covert genocide. Choosing a life of crime and knowing what is at stake is not living an abundant life at all. Some of us are merely existing with no real purpose in our life (Luke 12).

Can you imagine if we could stop the Black-on-Black crime in the United States. There would be no need to continue to build more penitentiaries around the country, The government makes an enormous amount of money from mass incarcerations throughout the states. The justice department makes a good living having grown men who have issues following rules in the free world. There are a lot of men who have a hard time humbling themselves to follow the rules and regulations established by your parents, or the authority on your, job, and school. Black people are one of the biggest contributors to the revenue generated in the United States. Yet every other culture, race of people can come to the United States and own land, secure bank loans, investments and generate wealth from our Black dollars. And many of us are born and raised in the United States and don't own anything or land of our own. It really is a sad commentary that many Black people that live here. We do not know what is important or know how to come together, to build something in the U.S. we can call our own. Our priorities are out of order. We are more eager to compete against each other, which ultimately keeps black people divide.

Many of us want to genuinely do the right thing; but for some of us when our backs are against the wall, we are going to do what is necessary to survive. Sometimes our bad habits come with bad decisions and with serious consequences. Our ancestors and forefathers' faith in the Lord is what got many of us through the tough times of slavery and the segregation of generations ago. Their lives should be an example; we all should follow--how their faith in God guided them through their trials and tribulations and difficult barriers of discrimination.

We have been deceived by what is truth and what is false. I don't think back then, the slaves had time to be using drugs because they would not be physically able to have worked in the fields—otherwise risk getting beat to death. Today many of us have addictions that have kept us from being a good father to our children, a responsible man, and a good husband. Many of our addictions, has to do with our desire to stop, and only God can save us. Many of us are not tired of letting our habits, lifestyles control and run our lives yet. May it be drugs, alcohol, prostituting, or hustling, robbing etc. You cannot serve two Masters (Matthew 6:24).

Drugs are destroying a lot of people today. Opioids and fentanyl are taking people out at an alarming rate—more than crack did in the 1980s and 90s. Drugs was another way that the government allowed us to hang ourselves. Look at all the time in a person's life—wasted years and nothing to show for it. Drugs has kept many fathers and men out of position to pursue their goals and dreams. And being the male leader in the home for their spouse and children. It is easier for some men to run instead of dealing with their issues head on like a real God-fearing man would do. Many men do not understand when you learn how to talk to God; that He will show you how to be a strong man for your community and for your household. But the sad fact is that God is not real enough to many men. They are too busy walking in their egos and own strength—until they get sick and tired (Psalms 145). Deliver us from Evil

Identity Crisis

There are many men who do not understand how important and why they are so vital to their families and communities. Society has tried to dummy down and agitate men to stand in their positions and roles as fathers, husbands, and heads of households. One way is by pushing them to believe it is not necessary to be there for their significant other and children. There is not enough male role models and influencers for young men growing up in these tough times. Especially in the Black community. There is a huge absence of Dad's that are not actively involved in their children's lives. Consequently, you have a lot of young Blacks and young children growing up and not knowing how to be real men without having female like tendencies and behaviors.

Some men have severe self esteem problems and issues of being confident in themselves. This causes problems regarding interacting and building relationships with other people. Some men do not think that they are special or good enough to be in a great place in life. The devil will always lie to you to keep you from taking hold of the promises that God has made to us. Many men cannot believe or are not made aware that they are fearfully and wonderfully made in

God's image. The Lord has put something unique and different in all of us. This has set you apart from everyone else (Psalms 139: 13-18).

Lacking the understanding that God has made you in His image makes you unaware of who you really are and the greatness within you. Not knowing your assignment or purpose on this earth is one issue; but not knowing who you are as God's creation here in this world is another. Not knowing who you are is an identity crisis (Ephesians 2:8-10). It is not enough just to know about your ethnicity and history; but you need to know specifically why God allowed you to be birthed into this world. We waste so much valuable time pursuing visions and dreams that are not our true purpose. God created us; but it seems like He is always left out of our plans, goals, and dreams. We must realize that God is our manufacturer. He has the complete manual for us (Jeremiah 1:1-5); (Galatians 1:11-5): (Matthew 6: 31-34).

Some men do not know much about a relationship with God. They barely know little about themselves other than their age, ethnicity, and place of birth (Genesis 1:26-28); (Genesis2:7-8); (John 1:1-1). Identity Crisis is what a lot of men are experiencing through life. Not aware of who you are, trying to figure out why you think the way you do, why you do certain things; and behave a certain way? There are so many people who do not know much about their dad. Would love to know more details about him, spend time with him, talking and experiencing the expression of love from their dad.

Some of us as adults grew up not having any closure. Many people find it hard to release the past because they never were able to get any closure. Closure to be at peace about things—to move forward. Unable to move forward stunts your growth. Not able to talk about the disappointment, abandonment, and rejection you felt from your father is where you will start your deliverance and healing process. It starts with being honest with yourself; and honest with your dad who hurt you. If they are no longer here, you can express it unto God in prayer. Sometimes the pain is too hard for men to talk about the painful experiences. Back in the old days some folks took their secrets and pains to the grave. Embarrassed and hurt to let the children know the whole story of various events in the family (Psalms 27:10-14).

The Lord has left some principles and spirituals laws for us to follow while we are here in this world (Joshua 1:7-9). The devil has another agenda for people in this world—and that is to steal, kill, and destroy us. The devil finds unique and creative ways to blind us from various truths and realities. He does this so we can continuously make bad choices. For us to be free to fulfill our purpose in this world. We need to repent and ask God for forgiveness. You can not carry anger and unforgiveness in your heart. Holding anger and unforgiveness is an easy doorway for the devil to come in and destroy you. The devil will lie to you and say you are not ready for change yet. There are countless men in the bible that the Lord used who had flaws. God knows and left the Holy Spirit to dwell in us to empower us to live victoriously (1 John 1:9); (Matthew 12:43-45); ((Acts 1:1-8).

In order to be a good leader, example, and role model to our children, wives; and communities you must be secure in yourself. Some men do not want this because they do not want to be held accountable for their behavior. Afraid what people will say and think. Your children are watching you and as they get older—they are going to remind you of how terrible of an example you were to them. God has left a responsibility to us as fathers, husbands, and brothers. You must stand before God and answer to him when its all over in the end. God is going to ask you—why you did not fulfill the obligations here on earth (2 Corinthians 5:3-10).

We spend all our time in the world trying to build our muscles up—meanwhile, what about your inner man. Building up your inner man is more important and where you will find true peace also. Insecurities and lack of peace has left a lot of people with an empty space within wondering and searching for closure. Having peace of mind to be able to identify what your father was like as a man living in this world. We are comforted by God to move on; but these question marks remain until you hear from other family members. Family members who were there and could speak on certain respects of your father's life. Questions of who, what, when, and why—of family secrets were always kept quiet. Evil; wicked deeds were held in a dark secret place to avoid exposing individuals past wicked lifestyles.

When you have knowledge concerning the past of the matriarchs of your family—you feel like you have more sense of belonging in this world, instead of feelings of just existing. Some insecurities take root within some of us as a child of feeling abandoned and left out. Especially when you have activities, holidays; and events where both parents are usually involved. As a child you may have questions that you really do not know how to ask your mother.

Having a father or male figure demonstrating leadership skills, providing for the family, and being responsible; and protecting the family helps you to grow and transition into adulthood as a man. A woman can not really teach a boy how to be a man because she has never been a man before to identify and explain certain things to her son. On the other hand, there are a lot of fathers in the home with the mothers who have not always been good examples either. There are many single parent homes these days where mothers are holding down both responsibilities as mom and dad.

This has been going on for years; but back in those times children were more respectful. There was more structure and discipline. The government was not telling parents how they should discipline and raise their children. Calling the police on your parents was not even an option when I was being raised by my parents. It is a different time now. So many men came up short leaving the home for many reasons. The absence of the father in the home has left a lot of young men without examples of real men to follow.

This is why there are some men who act like women in the way they say and do things. Being around women all the time has caused some men to take on a lot of female characteristics and tendencies. Because no male figure is around constantly to impact that young man's life. With a lot of men out of position in the home it has left empty spaces and many voids in a lot of men lives. It leaves an unforeseen void that opens the door for some insecurities to invade their lives.

Without the proper training and teaching from the leadership in your life and in the home—you are not going to be secure within yourself to face various challenges that confront you in life. Being unprepared weakens our self esteem and confidence as men. It is essential for young boys to have structure in the home growing up. This is very important to enable you to have the discipline necessary to take on various responsibilities as a man. With proper leadership, guidance, and direction—fatherhood and becoming an husband should not be an overwhelming situation of having a family one day.

There are so many men still trying to figure out who am I? Trying to be who people want you to be leaves you lost as to who you really are. When you seek approval from people—this is what people pleasers do. They are more secure in other people's opinion than their own. Some of us have carried that pain, feeling of abandonment, and rejection inside of us from childhood to the present unknowingly. When I say unknowingly, I mean that some of us have carried a lot of unresolved pain and issues since childhood that you have become immune to those things. These traits and pains are still there because they have never been resolved. Some men are assaulting and killing women and children when they can not get their way. Mature stable men do not behave like this.

Mental Health

There is an epidemic of mental health issues and emotional disorders today. People who are so emotional and have been out of control, assertive, and aggressive-- most of the time feel or believe that certain people or specific individuals are out to get them. This is why they become overly defensive and aggressive because they feel people will try to harm them and they are afraid of being hurt, abandoned or rejected. Again. They believe that people do not love them or care about them all the time. They are extremely sensitive people.

Sometimes the demonic spirit of self-pity destroys people mind to the point that you are not independently capable of being emotionally secure on your own. So these individuals depend on other people to make them feel special or think good things about themselves. So, from day to day of these interactions with people they become disorganized and mentally frustrated with themselves.

This is why a lot of our young people who grow up in difficult home settings become suicidal, depressed, and commit suicide. And you have some people who were by God's grace able to keep a sound mind to make it through those challenges growing up in a bad environment. For them to make it through on a daily basis they have to fight vigilantly to keep a sound mind. They gravitate or pick up on certain habits to enable them to sustain themselves from self-pity and low self-esteem.

Have you ever wondered how a woman could sell her body and then take the money back to her pimp. Satan is the king of all pimps. He is a master manipulator, liar, and impersonator. A lot of people are being pimped and prostituted by Satan but do not realize it. He is stealing your dignity and self-worth in exchange for material possessions and a need to look and feel special (John 1).

You must be willing to renew your mind daily because there are oppositions daily, we deal with emotionally as people. Some people have been robbed of their emotional stability. The ole cliché, "you've lost your mind"; is true for some. But God's word can renew your mind. For some people it does not mean that you need a mental health evaluation in every situation of some kind. But realize and know that there are times that you must reevaluate and get yourself back in order. Maybe it is spiritual or demonic activity or suffering loss of a loved one. Experiencing grief is normal with these circumstances. Sometimes burden down with a lot; we could use that support and encouragement. We all have been through time when a Spirit of Discouragement has attacked us. Through someone spirituals prayers and encouragement ministering to us helped break those yokes off us at that time. Galatians 6:1-6

Excessive grief is carrying things uncontrollably and continually out of control. This is when abnormal or unusual behavior starts taking place. Self-pity is excessive self-absorbed unhappiness over one's own troubles. Pity for oneself especially a self-indulgent dwelling on one's own sorrows or misfortunes. Your self-pity can make it hard to appreciate that other people face more serious troubles than you do. Especially exaggerated or self-indulgent pity where you believe that you are the victim who has done no wrong (2 Corinthians 4:4; Isaiah 26:3; 2 Corinthians 10:5; Psalms 94:11).

Damages during your childhood and young adulthood can cause a person to be excessively self-indulgent. Some healing must take place before the deliverance process. You see a lot of insecurities about ourselves have stunted our growth into adulthood as men. External changes are continuously happening around us; while inwardly and mentally we are stuck on pause by internal mental traumas we are trying to figure out and deal with. Your relationships with people are fragile because the least little thing will offend you and cause you to overreact, another thing we will have to do for change and deliverance is to repent and turn from our wicked ways.

God can transform and change anybody. There is no sin too great that the Lord is not willing to forgive us. He is not like man who holds grudges. He is faithful and able to forgive us from all unrighteousness.

There are many men in the bible who had flaws. While you were in your mother's womb God knew every chapter in your life. He knew you would be in your current situation today. He knows our every thought. He created us. It was not a mistake that you were born in this world. God is real today and forever more.

Bipolar, schizophrenia, manic depression, ADHD, anxiety, and depression are just a few of the mental health issues people are facing today. Some of these mental health issues should be addressed sooner than later to keep people from accepting these emotions as normal. The devil will try to keep us in bondage through fear after we have experienced traumatic chain of events in our lives. Everyone deals with grief, trauma, and loss differently; but we as believers must exercise our God given power and ability and authority over people that are yoked up in bondage as the Lord has commanded us (Mark 9:22-28). There are some issues a psychiatrist just will not be able to help some people with--. It is out the scope of their practice, so they just medicate you to cope until you forget to take your medication. This means your problem still exist, but when God sets you free, your free indeed(1 Corinthians 2: 10-16/John 8:34-47)

Recognizing Your Insecurities

You know I have discovered that unhappiness and insecurities work hand and hand. Being able to recognize when you are unhappy is very important. Knowing when your mind is being attacked by the devil keeps you healed and delivered. Gods word will let you know immediately where that thought is coming from. If you do not address that thought, you will have a yoke of bondage wrapped around you unknowingly. All the lies and wiles to have you turn against yourself is what will happen. Those thoughts will try to cause you to feel inadequate about yourself, full of doubts and fears that will stagnate you and keep you standing in place for a long time. If you ask each of us what is happiness. We will probably have many different answers. Everyone may define love probably with the same results. But when you are doing a daily self-evaluation—where we all should do this regularly. Ask yourself two questions: are you happy right now about your life? And do I love me? How can I expect other people to love and care about me if I do not love and care about me?

The reason I compromise my happiness is because mines is more secure in other people's love and concern for me rather than my own. Fear of being alone or by yourself is not an option for some people. They need a crowd or entourage so they can feel special and loved by others. But it is really a mask or facade of how they really feel about themselves.

A big part of being secure is being able to love and accept who you are and how God created you in this world. How you appear to other people shouldn't be more important than how you see yourself. Can you look in the mirror at yourself with pleasure and love, or with hate and insecurities about yourself.

    A. Skin Color- Some feel like their skin is too dark, light, bumpy

    B. Height—Too short or not tall enough

    C. Weight—Too fat or too skinny

    D. Facial Features—Eyes, nose, or lips too big

    E. Popularity—Acceptance from peers

Those insecurities and self-images are the doorways that Satan uses to come into torment, oppress, or depress you—especially when something reminds you of that pain or feeling you experienced at that time. Self esteem grows within you when you're aware and knows what God says about you, and his purpose for creating you. (Romans 8:15-17) Once that revelation opens up to you, that as a believer in Christ you have the presence and power of God living on the inside of you; this will boost your confidence and esteem supernaturally. (Deuteronomy 28:13)

The devil attacks your weaknesses as a person and your value when your unaware of what God's word says about you. You begin to doubt who you are and what you can do. You are not secure as a man because your foundation was damaged during your childhood and young adulthood. Some healing must take place before the deliverance process. You will never be able to know who you are and your worth as a person until the chains are broken from you with total deliverance. The devil has stolen your identity, lied to you about your worth as a person, and has convinced you to believe all the negativity associated with you. (Philippians 4:13/Ephesians 2:10) Just remember God has a purpose and plan for your life. but we have to open our eyes and don't allow our insecurities to prevent us from walking in God's plan and purpose for our life. God bless you all who took the time out of your schedules to read and receive God's awesome words of deliverance. All of God's promises to us is in his word, this is what gives us power to walk in victory through any times. Who are you going to believe and trust in? It's your choice. Psalms146:6